GYMNASTICS

BALANCE BEAM

Tips, Rules and Legendary Stars

by Heather E. Schwartz

Consultant:
Julie Belemore
WA Senior Club Coach
Secretary Essex Gymnastics Association
BSGA Regional Judging Convenor

raintree
a Capstone company — publishers for children

Raintree is an imprint of Capstone Global Library Limited, a company incorporated in England and Wales having its registered office at 264 Banbury Road, Oxford, OX2 7DY – Registered company number: 6695582

www.raintree.co.uk
myorders@raintree.co.uk

Edited by Gena Chester
Designed by Bobbie Nuytten
Picture research by Kelly Garvin
Production by Tori Abraham
Printed in China.

ISBN 978 1 4747 2635 1
20 19 18 17 16
10 9 8 7 6 5 4 3 2 1

British Library Cataloguing in Publication Data
A full catalogue record for this book is available from the British Library.

Acknowledgements
We would like to thank the following for permission to reproduce photographs: Alamy Images/ SPUTNIK, 21; Capstone Press: Karon Dubke, 1, 8-9 (bottom), 10, 11, 12, 13, 16, 19 (top), 22, Martin Bustamante, 14, 15; iStockphoto/Brian McEntire, 6; Newscom: Angelo Cozzi Mondadori, 5, Jeff Siner/MCT, 28, Khalilov Yakov Itar-Tass Photos, 26, Paul Kitagaki Jr./ MCT, 27, Yang Zongyou Xinhua News Agency, 29; Shutterstock: 4Max, 15 (bottom), Aspen Photo, 17, 18, 23, 25, bikeriderlondon, cover, Jiang Dao Hua, 9 (top), Luigi Fardella, 24, prapass, 22, stefanolunardi, 19 (b), versh, 7

Every effort has been made to contact copyright holders of material reproduced in this book. Any omissions will be rectified in subsequent printings if notice is given to the publisher.

Contents

Making history
on the balance beam

At the 1976 Olympics, 14-year-old gymnast Nadia Comaneci performed a flawless **routine** on the balance beam. She'd already earned a perfect score on the uneven bars. Now she had another 10.0 score from the judges. That day she made history. She was the first woman ever to earn a perfect score in Olympic gymnastics.

Nadia inspired a new generation of young athletes. Girls all over the world were eager to try gymnastics, including the balance beam.

The balance beam is just as exciting and challenging for gymnasts today as it was when Nadia performed. It takes training and practice to conquer the event.

Fast fact:
The balance beam event falls under the category of artistic gymnastics. Other types of gymnastics include rhythmic, trampoline and sports acrobatics.

routine combination of skills performed in a gymnastics event

Nadia Comaneci competed for her home country of Romania in the 1976 Olympics.

Exclusive events

Only women compete in balance beam. Woman also perform in uneven bars, vault and floor exercise. Men compete in vault and floor exercise as well. Men also have their own events. The pommel horse, parallel bars, high bar and rings are events performed only by men. Overall, women compete in four events while men compete in six.

Chapter 1

Balance beam
basics

Gymnasts performing on the balance beam do jumps, poses and other skills. It's very similar to other gymnastic events except for one major difference. In balance beam, everything happens on a long, narrow plank. Challenging? Definitely!

Join the club

Want to try the balance beam event? You need a place to practise, the right equipment and qualified coaches. You can find all of these at a gymnastics club.

British Gymnastics is an organization that sets rules and runs programs for the sport in the United Kingdom. Member clubs must meet British Gymnastics' standards. You can find affiliated clubs near you on the British Gymnastics' official website.

Safety

Safety is the top priority in all gymnastics events. When performing on the beam, staying safe starts with the set-up. A regulation balance beam is constructed of a metal frame covered by a layer of foam and leather. The height can be adjusted for younger gymnasts.

Mats are placed around the beam to cushion gymnasts if they fall. Coaches and trainers are always nearby to help.

Fast fact:
The balance beam used at the Olympics is 10 centimetres (4 inches) wide and 5 metres (16.4 feet) long. It is 1.2 metres (4.1 feet) high.

5 metres long

10 centimetres wide

1.2 metres high

Getting started

Gymnasts who are new to the sport perfect their moves on the floor first. Learning skills on the floor helps gymnasts build confidence, strength and technique. When they jump, turn and flip through the air, they can use a line of tape on the mat and pretend it is a balance beam. On the mat, they can do this without fear. They don't have to worry about falling off the beam.

When gymnasts are ready, their coaches and trainers help them take their moves from the floor to the beam. They don't have to head straight for a high balance beam. There are lower beams available for practise. Lower beams give gymnasts even more time to build confidence and skills. They can progress from using practice equipment to working on a high balance beam.

Fast fact:
Low balance beams are as wide as high beams. Some lie right on the ground. Others are 15 to 18 centimetres (6 to 7 inches) off the ground.

Gymnasts need to be able to move and bend easily and comfortably. They need to wear clothing that is close fitting. If clothing is too baggy, coaches won't be able to tell if the gymnasts are in the right positions.

Most female gymnasts wear leotards for practice. Leotards are fitted and very stretchy. Gymnasts usually go barefoot but sometimes wear special gymnastics shoes. Socks and other kinds of shoes are too slippery to be safe.

Chapter 2

Tricks
to try

Once your coach decides you're ready, there are plenty of skills to try out on the high beam. You start with learning **mounts** and basic skills before moving on to more advanced moves.

Mounting the beam

Moves look amazing on a regulation high beam. Before gymnasts try these moves, they have to mount the balance beam. Scrambling up awkwardly won't impress anyone. But mounting the beam doesn't have to be complicated either. Basic mounts work just as well as more difficult ones.

Front support mount

Stand facing the side of the beam. Put your palms on the beam and grip the far edge with your fingers. Push down and jump up, extending one leg over to straddle the beam.

mount to get up on the balance beam or other gymnastics apparatus

Leg swing mount with half turn

Stand parallel to the beam on your left side. Step your left foot forward and place your left arm on the beam. Swing your right leg forward and up over the beam. At the same time, twist your body 180 degrees, so both hands are on the beam. You will end up straddling the beam in the opposite direction to where you began.

Dismounts

The dismount is just as important as the mount. In competition, it's even more important because it's the last move judges see. Gymnasts perform jumps, twists and flips as they dismount the beam. When they land, they have to stick it. This means they have to land on their feet with no extra steps once they hit the mat.

Forward walk

Stand on the beam with your hands on your hips. As you step forward, keep your knees straight. Swing your foot slightly out to the side of the beam. Point your toe and place it on the beam in front of you.

Relevé walk

Stand on the beam with your hands on your hips. Lift your heels so that you are up on your toes. As you step forward, keep your knees straight. Place your foot directly in front of you onto the beam.

Fast fact:
Relevé is French for "raised". Gymnasts and dancers use this word to describe raising their heels.

You need more than strength to perform well on the beam. You also need **flexibility**. You can build flexibility by doing stretches at home and in the gym. A hurdle stretch works the muscles at the back of your thigh. This basic stretch is one that every gymnast should do regularly. Here's how to do it.

1. Warm up your muscles with 10 to 15 minutes of **cardiovascular** exercise, such as walking or jogging.

2. Sit with one leg extended in front of you. The other should be bent with your foot on your thigh and your knee pointing out. Point your toes and reach up with your arms as high as you can.

3. Lean forward, keeping your back straight and stomach tight. Go as low as you can while keeping the correct position.

4. Hold for 10 to 15 seconds. Lift back up so that your arms are reaching high again. Flex your toes.

5. Repeat two to three times and switch legs.

flexibility ability to bend or move easily
cardiovascular relating to the heart and blood vessels

Backward walk

Stand on the beam with your hands on your hips. Keep your knees straight as you step backward. Swing your foot slightly out to the side of the beam. Feel for the top of the beam with your toes. When you find it, place your foot down and continue.

More advanced moves

As gymnasts gain experience, they can perform impressive and stylish skills on the balance beam. They can even go airborne!

Handstand

Look down at the beam as you step forward and bend at the waist. Place your hands on the beam, keeping your arms straight. Keeping your legs straight, kick them up and together.

Wolf jump

Swing your arms to create momentum and jump straight up. While in the air, bend one leg under your body. Stretch the other straight in front of you.

Free walkover

Push off with one leg while kicking the other behind you.
Arching your back, flip forward and land feet first on the beam.

Fast fact:
Gymnasts dust chalk on their hands and legs to get a better grip on equipment. The powder absorbs sweat.

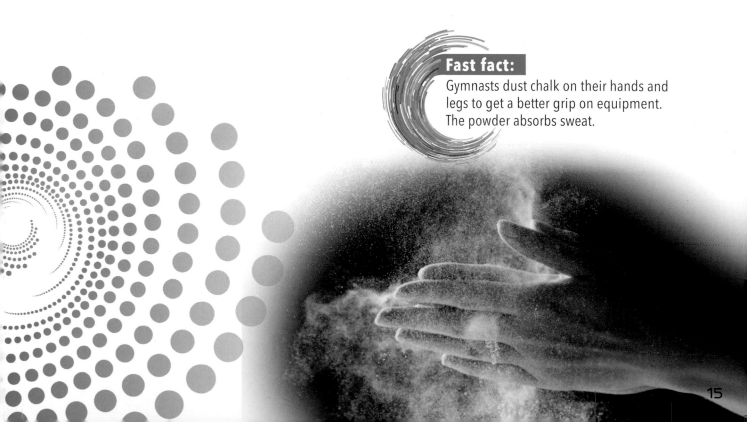

Chapter 3

Meet to
compete

Gymnastics competitions give gymnasts a chance to challenge themselves. They can reach for new goals and even win medals. British Gymnastics has numerous levels based on a gymnast's age, discipline and goals.

Gymnasts can start in the organization's FUNdamentals program when they are just a year old. FUNdamentals focuses on teaching young children how to move their bodies. At this level there are no competitions. Performances are centred around having fun

With each level, gymnasts gain experience and skills. Eventually they may compete as **elite** athletes. In elite programs, gymnasts train for competitions such as the British Championships, the World Championships and the Olympic Games.

Gymnasts have their performance scored in competition. Judges use a rule book called a Code of Points. When judging gymnasts on beam, they look at form, height of aerial moves and execution of moves. They also note the **artistry** in the routine.

A new system at the elite level gives gymnasts one score for the difficulty of their routine. A second score deducts points for mistakes made in execution. The scores are combined to create a final score.

elite the best
artistry creative skill

Pulling it all together

Gymnasts who plan to compete combine several balance beam moves into a routine. Balance beam routines are generally about 70 to 90 seconds long. It doesn't sound like much time, so every moment is critical. Judges watch to make sure gymnasts don't go over the time limit.

Putting together a great routine is a balancing act. Gymnasts need to include skills they know they can perform well. They also need to include moves that will impress judges and earn a high score.

Where should you turn when you're eager to compete? Your coach, of course! He or she can help you plan a routine that will show off your skills and meet the requirements for your level of competition.

Pack your gym bag

Don't leave home without important things to get you through the event. Make sure you pack:

- healthy snacks
- a water bottle
- deodorant
- any equipment you need to protect you from injury, such as wrist guards or athletic tape
- hairspray, gel and hair bands to keep hair pulled back in a bun or plait
- a tracksuit to keep you warm while waiting to perform

Fast fact:

British Gymnastics requires long hair to be pulled back and away from your face during competition. Some coaches may have additional rules about the types of clips you're allowed to use. Be sure to check the rules before the competition.

Performance technique

The world's best gymnasts go beyond displaying their technical skill in competition. They **choreograph** balance beam routines that show style and artistry to present themselves as talented performers as well as accomplished athletes. Oksana Omelianchik was 15 years old when she won a gold medal at the 1985 European Championships. Her performance was practically flawless and fun to watch. Here's why.

- She used the whole beam. Poses and positions are important, but Oksana performed many moves that took her back and forth across the beam as well.

- She varied her skills throughout the routine. She mixed up moves to perform poses, then flips, then poses and then leaps. The variety created a fast-paced routine. She didn't give her audience a chance get bored.

- She included both easier and more difficult skills in her routine. It was challenging but not to the point that it caused her a lot of stress.

- Instead of looking tense or worried, she appeared to be relaxed, confident and enjoying herself. The audience could relax and enjoy the performance too.

choreograph to create and arrange movements that make up a routine

Oksana Omelianchik was only 15 years old when she competed at the 1985 European Championships.

Chapter 4

Practice
makes perfect

Gymnasts often train for years before deciding to compete. When you're preparing for a competition, be sure to take your time. The amount of time you spend training for a competition is usually up to your coach. He or she can help you create a schedule and make sure you are prepared to compete.

The last week before competition is a good time to perfect your moves. You can also practise exactly what you will experience during the competition. For example, you might want to wear a number while you practise. You could try warming up for the amount of time you will be allowed at the competition.

Practice will help you feel much more comfortable when it's competition day. Working closely with your coach as you train and prepare will help relieve stress too.

See yourself succeed

A great deal of time is spent on physical preparation before a competition. But there are plenty of things a gymnast can do to prepare mentally for a competition as well. **Visualization** helps many gymnasts ease anxiety. Here's how it works. Run through your routine in your mind. Focus carefully on the moves you plan to perform, and then imagine yourself performing each of them perfectly. See yourself earning a high score. Allow yourself to feel happy and proud. Visualization can build your confidence and help you relax, which makes you more likely to succeed.

Positive thinking helps in a similar way. Be your own biggest fan. Replace negative thoughts with positive ones. Tell yourself you can do it.

Eating healthy foods and getting enough sleep helps you prepare both physically and mentally. You need energy and rest in order to perform well, but you also need these things to handle the stress of competition.

visualization act of imagining or forming a mental picture

Chapter 5
Balance beam
legends

Nadia Comaneci and Oksana Omelianchik are not the only gymnastics legends to leave their mark on the balance beam. Gymnasts throughout history and around the world have shaped what it means to perform in the event.

Olga Korbut

In 1969 at the Soviet Union's national championships, Olga Korbut was the first gymnast to perform a backward aerial somersault on the balance beam.

Olga won a gold medal in balance beam for the Soviet Union at the 1972 Olympic Games. She won a silver medal in balance beam at the 1976 Games. She is best known, however, for her originality in gymnastics. Performing new moves, like the backward aerial somersault on the beam, influenced athletes and judges to think differently about what gymnasts can accomplish in the sport.

Beijing 2008 ᴏᴏᴏᴏᴏ

Shawn Johnson

Shawn Johnson started doing gymnastics when she was three years old. She trained for the Olympics for years. But while practising on the beam at the 2008 Games, her routine didn't go very well. She just couldn't get it right.

When her big moment came, her training kicked in. She impressed the judges with her strength and confidence as well as her ability to perform a difficult dismount. At 16 she took home an Olympic gold medal for the United States and became known throughout the world as a champion.

Deng Linlin

Deng Linlin started gymnastics when she was five years old. She trained hard for years. At times family members wanted her to quit or at least slow down. But Linlin did not want to stop.

In 2012 she competed at the London Olympic Games. She fell while performing on the balance beam in a team event. Her mistake cost her team a medal.

A few days later, she had a chance to redeem herself. She performed on the beam as an individual athlete. Her routine included front flips, back flips, aerials and difficult leaps. This time she impressed the judges and took home an Olympic gold medal for China.

Simone Biles

Simone Biles started gymnastics when she was six years old. She worked hard, training and competing for many years. By the time she was 18, she was practising at least 32 hours each week.

In 2015 she made history. She became the first woman ever in her sport to win three all-around World titles in a row. She had 10 World Championship gold medals in total, including two for balance beam.

Fast fact:
Women couldn't win individual medals in Olympic gymnastics until 1952.

Becoming a legend on the balance beam takes strength, style and a great deal of determination. Just like you, these legendary gymnasts all started by learning the basics. Practice and hard work will bring you closer to achieving your gymnastics dreams.

Glossary

artistry creative skill

cardiovascular relating to the heart and blood vessels

choreograph to create and arrange movements that make up a routine

elite the best

flexibility ability to bend or move easily

mount to get up on the balance beam or other gymnastics apparatus

routine combination of skills performed in a gymnastics event

visualization act of imagining or forming a mental picture

Read more

Gymnastics (Mad about), J. Heneghan (Wayland, 2016)

The Gymnastics Book: The Young Performer's Guide to Gymnastics, Elfi Schlegel and Claire Ross Dunn (Firefly, 2012)

The Science Behind Gymnastics (Science of the Summer Olympics), L.E. Carmichael (Raintree, 2016)

Websites

www.british-gymnastics.org
Find a club near where you live and take a look at the profiles of your favourite British gymnasts.

www.fig-gymnastics.com
Find all of the official rules of gymnastics at the official website of the Fédération Internationale de Gymnastique.

www.ukgymnastics.org
Find out all the latest news about gymnastics in the United Kingdom.

Index